The whole life of the church benefits from the mysterious and powerful help of angels.
> —Catechism of the Catholic Church, 334

I wish there was a way to tell parents of children who have been abused that their children are surrounded by angels to protect them…
> —Client reflecting on her childhood abuse

HELD CLOSE
BY AN ANGEL

HELD CLOSE BY AN ANGEL

Chrisanna Harrington

*A Guide for Survivors of
Childhood Trauma Who Find
Themselves Single Again*

Tate Publishing & *Enterprises*

Held Close by an Angel
Copyright © 2011 by Chrisanna G. Harrington MA, RD/LD, NCC, LMHC.
All rights reserved.

No part of this publication may be reproduced, stored in a retrieval system or transmitted in any way by any means, electronic, mechanical, photocopy, recording or otherwise without the prior permission of the author except as provided by USA copyright law.

All scripture quotations, unless otherwise indicated, are taken from the Holy Bible, *New International Version*®. NIV®. Copyright © 1973, 1978, 1984 by International Bible Society. Used by permission of Zondervan. All rights reserved.

This book is designed to provide accurate and authoritative information with regard to the subject matter covered. This information is given with the understanding that neither the author nor Tate Publishing, LLC is engaged in rendering legal, professional advice. Since the details of your situation are fact dependent, you should additionally seek the services of a competent professional.

Scripture is taken from the New King James Version and the New American Standard

The opinions expressed by the author are not necessarily those of Tate Publishing, LLC.

Published by Tate Publishing & Enterprises, LLC
127 E. Trade Center Terrace | Mustang, Oklahoma 73064 USA
1.888.361.9213 | www.tatepublishing.com

Tate Publishing is committed to excellence in the publishing industry. The company reflects the philosophy established by the founders, based on Psalm 68:11,
"The Lord gave the word and great was the company of those who published it."

Book design copyright © 2011 by Tate Publishing, LLC. All rights reserved.
Cover design by Amber Gulilat
Interior design by Joel Uber

Published in the United States of America

ISBN: 978-1-61739-662-5
1. Religion; Counseling
2. Psychology; Developmental, Adulthood & Aging
11.02.10

Dedicated to the Angel that prompted me
to feel and understand what it means to heal.

Thank you to Stuart Stuthers MS, NCC, LMHC, my supervisor, who helped in making this book clinically sound and reader friendly.

Thank you to Dr. Eduardo Carmona-Gonzales, MD who edited the chapter on suicide.

Thank you to Robert V. Christiansen for his tireless editing efforts.

Thank you to Cara, my daughter, who with me makes a complete loving family and reminds me to continue to walk in this journey, with Christ!

Table of Contents

Foreword	11
Introduction	15
Family of Origin	19
Adult Children	25
All That Negativity	29
Word Manipulation	33
Inspired by Madame Butterfly	37
Suicide	43
Healing Past Hurts	49
Current Relationships	57
Forgiveness	61
Attract to Your Level of Individuation	67
Love	71
Myth of Eros and Psyche	77
Moving Forward	85
Closing	109
Glossary	113
Bibliography	115

Foreword

*For He will give His angels charge concerning you,
To guard you in all your ways.*

PSALM 91:11

It can be a difficult and painful process for the adult survivor of childhood abuse to recognize, face, and work through the long term and sometimes debilitating hardship and suffering that was experienced. Strong emotions such as emptiness, confusion, and sadness often surface as the adult survivor realizes that the sacred trust and innocence of their childhood was irreparably broken, that these experiences cannot be erased, and that the residual personal and social dysfunction is carried into adulthood. Once childhood abuse is recognized and faced, healing begins with restoration of hope, resolution of grief, new understanding, and positive changes in behavior. *Held Close by an Angel* will serve as a helpful starting point and guide for those who are willing to explore and recognize the impact of childhood abuse and its resulting trauma in their lives. It will help the reader face and reflect on many of the relevant issues of recovery and begin the healing process so that a healthier, more stable, and fulfilling lifestyle can be realized.

In *Held Close by an Angel*, Chrisanna Harrington merges traditional mental health concepts and information with orthodox Christian values to create a spiritual foundation for lasting healing. Within this context, Chrisanna introduces the reader to the concepts of Inner Child and Adult Child and explains how abuse and trauma experienced during childhood carry into the Adult Child's personality and social functioning by retaining experiences, feelings, and beliefs as they were experienced in childhood. While specific emphasis and spiritual context is provided for Christians who find themselves single, this book will also serve as useful guidance for *any* reader who is married or involved in a dysfunctional or abusive relationship where the goal is to bring an end to the abuse, gain emotional strength, and heal from the damage.

Chrisanna courageously reveals portions of her own personal struggle of recovery and reconciliation through narratives at the beginning of each chapter. Therein you will find the essence of her spiritual foundation and walk with God, her human struggle, her story of angelic healing and guidance, and the basis of her recovery from childhood abuse and trauma. Chrisanna is an esteemed colleague and personal friend. Her recovery has served as the impetus for her dynamic lifework as a specialist in the treatment of childhood trauma. This book, and her story, is a testament to her grace and soul-driven desire to help others regain hope, muster courage, and heal from these difficult challenges.

—Stuart A. Stuthers, MS, LMHC, NCC

Introduction

At fifty years of age, I would expect that I would have a full understanding of myself as a human being. I would also expect that after thirty of those fifty years, walking with Christ, I would be changed, a new person in Christ and all the struggles of my human upbringing would be "worked out." Why is it then that I keep struggling with the same issues? If I am a new creature in Christ, then I am permanently changed, and if I am walking in Christ, I am whole. This is all true and biblically based for my spirit; the clincher is that we are still human and still struggle with the Inner Child inside that never healed, or is partially healed and God allows situations to trigger emotions that are still "raw." We react to them as adults and then feel shame and humiliation. All is not lost, because this is just where God wants us to be in order to heal. The parts that are not under wraps will keep surfacing in instances of miscommunication. Healing the inner child takes more than a baptism, more than a faith prayer. Healing the Inner Child has to do with looking at ourselves and identifying behaviors, attitudes, and personal struggles that prevent us from having healthy relationships with our spouses or ex-spouses, children, friends, and significant others.

The traumas from childhood that are buried deep inside are the things that eventually seep out if not dealt with, when boundaries start to slide. The traumas from childhood manifest themselves in inappropriate ways such as yelling, slamming doors, walling yourself off from your family or friends, walking away from significant relationships, or finding yourself deep in an addiction of sex, food, pornography, alcohol, or drugs. The trauma may not be something earth shattering, in fact, some people do not see any trauma at all. It was, however, a shift from a nurturing environment that left holes in the soul, resulting in feeling "less than" or "better than." The lack of normal development resulted in an Adult Child not having the ability to be authentic in his/her relationships; what was happening on the inside was not congruent with the persona presented on the outside.

As you will see, there is the Holy Spirit that takes into account our hope and belief in a new, peaceful life. For many, there is still the unhealed Inner Child that does not change if the person has no insight into how he/she is being perceived or how he/she interacts with others. The personality is shaped in the formative years, and if there is trauma, the person will have repercussions throughout his/her life. If the feelings are not identified, expressed, or affirmed the dysfunction will continue throughout life.

Changes in the thought process need to be made dealing with establishing new behaviors that are healthy.

It is my hope in this book to shed some light on healthy and unhealthy relationships. I want to look at healing the child in you that still cowers for fear of getting hit when someone is "yelling." Or the person who cannot trust because of memories when he/she trusted before and was left abandoned and crushed. For the person who feels "unworthy" and is unable to seek closeness and intimacy. For the person who would rather eat than express his/her anger. For the woman or man who does not want to lose weight for fear of having to be sexual. For the woman or man who cannot find true intimacy with his/her spouse because of feeling "dirty" or worthless due to sexual abuse as a child. For the man or woman who does not know that there are nice people in this world who do not want to take advantage of and destroy them. For the person who is extremely perfect, has done everything right, and becomes judgmental of others' humanity. It is for these people who feel slightly defective even though they know they are saved by Grace and are perfect in God's eyes that I am writing this book. If you are one of these broken human beings or you know someone like this, please read on. You will have more understanding and find that people who have suffered greatly can appreciate greatly and love greatly when they feel safe and their Inner Child is healed. I also believe that much of the reason we have made it this far has to do with heavenly creatures protecting us. The protection keeps us here so that we have some years to feel whole, heal, and experience this earth as God intended. We can experience this life as He created us, before all the negative stuff, the abuse that altered our lives in ways that were unpredictable by our human minds. This is a guide for Christians who find themselves in midlife without a partner. Your first or second or third marriage maybe did not work out. You are finding that you are single again, and just do not want to go through the process of getting into a new relationship without identifying what areas in your life need healing. You must identify your needs and what is a healthy relationship for you. My hope in this book is to help unlock the power of the Holy Spirit in you, to allow yourself to be vulnerable to God, and to trust that He sends Heavenly Angels to hold you close when you are feeling most abandoned. To give you hope for your future.

Also note that the stories told about "my clients" are not of a particular person. However, these are blended versions of life experiences of many people. They are used to illustrate points of healing.

Family of Origin

*You received a spirit of adoption as sons
through whom we cry: Abba! Father!*
ROMANS 8:15

I was not looked after or nurtured. I am sure that they thought they loved me. I am sure that the thought never entered their minds that this little life that was born to this family of four was to be neglected and tormented, to be the "toy" to inflict all their emotional pain in forms of physical and emotional abuse. It just happened, and it was a way of life. No one called it abuse back then. I was two, and the pain was too, too much to bear. I vaguely remember the little toddler girl with human bite marks all over her body from the neighborhood boy. How did I even get there? The three-year-old toddler who was sent out to get her brother from the backyard only to walk up to the baseball game behind the batter to get hit in the face with a baseball bat. What was I thinking! At three, I should have known how a baseball game worked! At a very young age I felt as if I were a nuisance for my family. As I grew up in that violent, unpredictable household, I would find myself hiding under my covers when the hitting and throwing of objects started. The days were times when my older brother and sister could play their sadistic games with me. The evening and nights were the times when my adolescent brother and sister would fight with my mother. The worst time was when my father was home between business trips and drunk. There always seemed to be a major physical altercation. Listening to arguing and beatings as I hid under my bed. I thought the violence would never reach me because I would never do anything to get a beating. My fear turned to numbness, the light in my little blue eyes faded, my heart stopped feeling joy…only when I read the picture bible that our pastor gave our family for Christmas one year did I feel peace. The picture of the Angel guiding the little boy and girl over the bridge was comforting to me. They were alone as I felt alone, yet had heavenly protection, and so did I. I could rest.

You may have grown up in a family that struggled in different ways. You may have been poor and so the whole mode of operation for your family was survival. You may have been from a wealthy family and not suffered from poverty; however, you may have suffered in other ways of expectations that were unrealistic. You may have been neither or in between; however, the stress that you and your family lived under was crushing, and there was no sense of peace, harmony, or hope in your environment. There are all sorts of ways that people suffer in their families of origin, and this suffering makes us who we are, both the positive and the negative.

Families of origin can be functional or dysfunctional. The word dysfunctional is used very readily these days. Let's first look at what a functional family provides. A functional family provides safety from the storm. A functional family is operating as a whole, and the thought of the future of all its members is taken into account. All members of a functional family have their needs met. This is a family that has good mental health, and they handle stress and losses as well as they are able to celebrate and find joy. This is a family that is able to allow the children to move out of the home and establish functional families of their own and build a great lineage.

Dysfunctional families are families where only one person is having his/her needs met. This may be the parent or teenager who is the addict, either through alcohol or drugs, legal or illegal, and the whole family is forced to meet the needs of the addict. Another example of one family member having his/her needs met is the person who is demanding about the family and puts undue stress on the family members. A dysfunctional family member can also be a spouse or parent who lives his/her life away from the family. He/she may prefer to be with others outside of the family so that his/her pretense is not readily recognized. The reason others outside the family are chosen is because a dysfunctional person finds it easier to put on a show for a brief period of time. Once the dysfunctional person returns to the home, he/she is free to drop the show and return to his/her normal dysfunction. This is the family where only one member is getting what they want and the other members have to walk on eggshells to try and prevent a disaster. An example of managing the stress would be the child who uses humor to redirect a raging parent. Or the wife who makes everything perfect for her husband so he will not find fault with her. She believes that all she has to do is be more perfect and her husband will be pleased. Then he will not belittle her; her secret hope is that he would realize the gift he has in his family.

These are examples of dysfunctional families. In both cases there is only one person having his/her needs met. In the example of the child, he or she is not having his/her nurturing needs met and he/she may grow up to have codependent behaviors. These children will grow up to be Adult Children because nurturing was lacking in the Family of Origin. They then developed unhealthy coping mechanisms to assure that they survived. In the case above, this child may use humor inappropriately, or not be able to show authentic emotions with his/her adult partner. Other examples of coping mechanisms include self-neglect, the development of survival instincts that prevent a person from establishing strong adult relationships. This happens when the survival instinct causes a person to be very independent and is unable to be interdependent with a partner or spouse. This is because he/she never knew safety and peace from the family in which he/she grew up.

The Adult Child never saw a family system that had the father and mother working together to meet their needs as a couple and the needs of the family in their roles as parents. Adult Children often would rather do things on their own and become fiercely independent, leaving their partner or spouse feeling very lonely. On the other hand, the Adult Child may become totally dependent, leaving the partner feeling trapped or suffocated.

In the example of the wife, she is not getting her needs met because there is no partnership in the relationship; all energies are generated toward the husband. She will continue to suppress her needs until she becomes numb. She most likely was an Adult Child going into the marriage not having the ability to realize her marriage was not the kind of marriage God intended for her. This happens to men as well, when the wife is the narcissistic one and the family revolves around her needs.

These are examples of both functional and dysfunctional families. When we mature as adults and experience pain, we can act out in the pain or we can feel the pain and move through it. C. S. Lewis writes in his book *The Problem of Pain* that we can allow God to chisel out godly character in us. In this next section we will look at the characteristics of Adult Children and what you can do to heal that Inner Child and become an adult in an adult body.

Adult Children

*For if our heart condemns us, God is greater than
our heart, and knows all things.*

1 JOHN 3:20

I wanted to make a difference in my children's lives. I did not want them to be neglected. I wanted them to feel self-worth, to know that God created them and had a plan for their lives. I wanted them to know that their mother and father loved them. My prayer for them as I carried them in my womb and as they grew up was this, "God please develop her mind, her spirit and body, and keep her on the straight and narrow path so that your plan for her will come to fruition!" I was never going to let any abuse happen. I was around them all the time; I left them only with someone I trusted and only when I needed to accompany my then husband to a function. I was always with them. No one would abuse my children; I became obsessed with being the perfect wife, the perfect mother, and making the perfect family. The only problem was that I was so busy looking out for physical or sexual abuse, I missed the overt emotional abuse from my then husband: the lying, the name calling, the feeling that we, a wife and daughters were a nuisance for him. The fear of being in a violent household was so entrenched in me that I did everything possible to be compliant to the point of allowing psychological abuse and neglect. I allowed my daughters to see that it was normal for their father to forget their mother's birthday, normal not to celebrate the wedding anniversary, normal for Valentine's Day to be a celebration by mother and daughters and not a time for the father to show his love for his wife or for his daughters. All the excuses, "he is just too busy," "Daddy has a lot of pressure with his job, we need to be supportive of him," etc. We were living a life to make life easier for my then husband, walking on eggshells around him as to not incite a rampage of slamming doors, kicking the dog and worse just before he left, kicking my daughter down the hall like an animal. We became needless and wantless. I passed the numbness on to my children. I was the target for all his jokes; not much had changed from my childhood, except the beating and alcohol were missing. I allowed my children to be in a home that was so oppressive, it is a wonder we are all still alive today.

∞

Let's look at the characteristics of Adult Children; who are we? We are people who are very hard on ourselves and we are people who try very hard in our lives; we have wonderful careers, and yet we struggle with intimacy in our personal relationships. Adult Children can be very good friends; however, in relationships in which they feel vulnerable they may not be able to connect for fear of being crushed or abused again. There are many books out on Adult Children, and here is a partial list of characteristics as described in John and Linda Friel's books. Adult Children are described to have some of the following symptoms:

1. Difficulty expressing emotions
2. Find emotional, sexual, or physical intimacy very difficult
3. Have a history of broken relationships
4. Difficulty getting out of abusive relationships
5. Difficulty handling compliments or criticism
6. Difficulty identifying their needs and/or meeting the needs of their partner
7. Difficulty saying "no"
8. Inability to be interdependent
9. Extreme dependence or extreme isolation
10. Difficulty playing or having fun
11. Diagnosis of anxiety/depression/phobias/panic
12. Obsessions and compulsions
13. Addictions: food, alcohol, drugs, exercise, work, or sex

14. Body system problems such as irritable bowel, migraines, sleep problems, tension

15. Poor or inflated self-esteem

16. Black-and-white thinking, all or nothing, no ability to see "gray"

Highlight or circle the characteristics that you see in yourself. It is healthy that you can see these parts of your life and your characteristics. That means that you can see yourself more clearly and most likely want to change.

Negative Self Talk

…for the Holy Spirit will teach you in that very hour what you ought to say.

LUKE 12:12

I was told that I was not a very bright girl. My parents did not expect too much out of me. Two weeks after turning five, I started kindergarten in September. I cried a lot. My brother and sister called me names and used me as a human punching bag. I talked fast and was nervous; they called me "Quicks-anna." My nose, from being broken at age three, was larger than normal; they called me "Chrisanna-Banana," before I knew it all the neighborhood kids called me either, "Quicks-Anna" or "Chrisanna-Banana." I did not believe in myself. How could I believe in myself? I remember asking my brother for help in math as a freshman in college and he told me I was an "idiot" and "you will never learn anything." He always told me I was a "slow learner." I am not sure how I even made it through undergraduate school. It was only by the grace of God. It was only because I had heavenly beings guiding me when I did not even recognize or even acknowledge the existence of God. God never gave up on me. He continued to woo me, to draw me closer and closer, and eventually I could define myself as God sees me. Because of the blood of Christ that is covering me, I could see myself in a positive light. He sees me as beautiful, intelligent, and loving, because I was made in His image.

Another aspect of being Adult Children is that we can carry with us the Negative Self Talk from childhood that limits our ability to achieve and express ourselves. If you struggle with Negative Self Talk, I challenge you to turn it around to Positive Self Talk. Become aware of just how often you say negative things about yourself or think the worst in any situation. When these negative, self-defeating thoughts come into your mind, *stop!* Remind yourself that you are a child of God, and God does not make mistakes! God is the Heavenly Father who would never give you "stones" when you ask for "bread." So let's do some practice:

Negative Self Talk: "I'm fat, and I hate myself!"

Positive Self talk: "I am feeling so overweight. I know that I have indulged; maybe it is time for me to seek professional help because I want to be healthy."

Negative Self Talk: "I am just a screw-up in relationships; I keep attracting the wrong type of person."

Positive Self Talk: "I want to look at my part in these relationships. What I feel is I want to have a supportive loving relationship. I trust that God will orchestrate the right person to come into my life. I will start to focus on myself becoming healthier so I can be ready for the next person God brings into my life."

Negative Self Talk: "I am acting just like my father; I must be destined to be this way!"

Positive Self Talk: "Why does this behavior feel so familiar? I know that what I want is to be able to express myself with words, not by slamming things around. When I start to feel the rage starting, I will remove myself from the situation, think about what I am feeling, and then act calmly to express my needs."

Now write down some situations in which you feel the negativity paralyzing you. Write down a negative thought that comes to mind and then "reframe" it to positive. Then dig a little deeper and ask yourself, "Who used to say that to me as a child?" That is the relationship that needs to heal. A trained therapist will be able to help you do this work.

Be gentle with yourself; cry about your losses or lost opportunities. Know that Jesus is catching every one of your tears. He has huge hands that can hold all of the waters of the world. (Psalm 89:25 "…I will set his hand over the sea, and his right hand over the rivers.") Know that Jesus is crying with you, because He has not planned all this suffering for you! "For know that the plans that I have for you, plans of peace and not of evil, to give you a future and a hope" (Jeremiah 29:11).

Word Manipulation

Death and life are in the power of the tongue...
Proverbs 18:21

I hated being lied to. Lying was something I vowed not to do. I am sure that I did my fair share of it; however, when I became an adult I knew that I did not like liars and I was not going to be one. I believed that if I gave my word then I needed to make good on that. I was the one who would give too much information too soon. I felt so broken that if I found someone who accepted me with all my faults, then I thought I was safe. Little did I know that when you share all your insecurities and are honest to a fault, those who do not have such noble plans can use that information to manipulate you. I was not safe at all; I just gave the man who was to become my husband material to control me. He was a very smart and manipulative man. I had no idea that I would marry and live a life that was all lies. That I would live in a home with a man who would not tell me the truth about himself. He was vague when I asked questions.

"Tell me Honey, what is it that is bothering you; how can I help you?" I would ask when he was detached. He would tell me it was only the "demons" in his mind. After fifteen years of marriage, I came to realize that my whole married life was a sham; he only married to have a cover for his other life. I felt desperately alone. The heavenly beings, the angels, they were there; even though I did not see them I could feel their presence. They were there to direct me, to bring people into my life to encourage me, and to help me to see through the lies. I had to cling desperately to God's word, which is always the truth.

Another survival mechanism for Adult Children is to manipulate words as a means of survival. If you take this into your newfound relationship, this can come back to hurt you. Your new relationship will find inconsistencies in your words and stories, and your credibility or trust level will decrease. Remember to keep your words true. When one's words are incongruent with one's actions, the words are *impotent*—they have no ability for action. I learned in my forties about the meaning of God's word. He *spoke* the *world* into being: "In the beginning God created the heavens and the earth. The earth was without form and void; and darkness was on the face of the deep. And the Spirit of God was hovering over the face of the waters. Then God *said*, 'Let there be light' and there was light" (Genesis 1:1-3). You can speak light into your world today.

Words are important; they can either build or destroy. Making sure that your words are congruent or can equal your actions is the sign of an adult. Being true to your word defines an adult who is comfortable with his/her personal image and can take responsibility for him/herself and others.

> "Creation is born of words which defeats nothingness and creates being" (The Word Among Us, June 2009 page 17).

You have the chance today, maybe for the first time, to create your life. If you feel you have nothing, then create something wonderful. But above all, always be true to your word.

Inspired by Cio Cio San, Madame Butterfly

I remember writing notes to my then husband telling him how wonderful he was and how much I loved him. I just wanted him to please forgive me for whatever I did that caused him to ignore me so much. I had no idea; I tried with all my might to be the Proverbs 31 woman. I saw him treat others so kindly in the community. I did not know what I did to be so ignored, to be made fun of, to feel like I was a nuisance. I made excuses: he was too tired, he had an important job, and he was under stress. Then there was the trip to Peru. It was a mission trip; my then husband went with a woman from his work. She came to pick him up at our home and drive to the airport. I went to give him a big hug and kiss as he was going to the car, to let him know I would miss him and would pray for him while he was on his trip. He turned away from me, with a look on his face, as if to tell me, I was a nuisance again…

My priest said to me, when my then husband and I separated, "This does not seem to be a marriage that God would want you in, and are you married more to the vow than you are to the man?" That I was. As an Adult Child, I was used to not having my needs met and giving everything to another, being dependent on that person to make decisions for me. I was not an equal part of the equation. Cio Cio San in Madame Butterfly is a famous example of a woman who had the best of intentions going into the marriage, only to find out after years of living in denial, that she was truly alone in the situation. She chose death; however, there is more that we can learn if we choose to change our circumstances through divorce and then allow God to work through our lives. We can allow God to chisel out that Christ-like character through the pain. Remember C. S. Lewis?

※

Okay, let's first look at what God wants for us in a marriage, "…man should leave his father and mother and cleave to his wife; and the two should become one flesh" (Matthew 19:5). This means that they are congruent with each other. They do not have to look or think alike; however, they will honor, accept and plan to be together. In Ephesians, this concept is illustrated through the famous wedding verse that a woman will be subject to her husband. There is a second part of this in Ephesians, and that is that a husband will love his wife as Christ loved the church. And how did Christ love the church? He laid down His life for her. (Ephesians 5:22-30) Okay, how many husbands or wives would put their life down for their spouse? I have witnessed this level of love and know that it can exist. You can make this level of love in your life if you choose to be with another person who is honoring you and has the capacity to care deeply for you, and you for them. You see, if a person hates his/her own flesh, how could he/she love and honor another? When you find your new partner and you see he/she has self respect you will be able to sense that he/she will respect you as well. It is then that you will have that honoring and loving connection.

Let's look at three simple qualities in a successful marriage or relationship:

1. *Affirmation:* The ability to communicate to your mate that he/she is special to you, valuable and an important part of your life.

2. *Affection:* The ability to be affectionate and touch, be sensual, and show physical connection.

3. *Appreciation:* After being able to show affirmation and affection, can a mate feel the appreciation from the other? Appreciating your mate is being able to identify all the ways that you respect him/her and honor him/her.

From not growing up with an example of what a healthy relationship looks like, Adult Children must look for what is healthy and what is normal in an adult relationship. It is normal to say good morning and good night. It is normal to have empathy given to you when you are sick or to give to your spouse or child when they are sick. It is normal to talk about your day without being judged. It is normal to make mistakes, ask for forgiveness and be forgiven. This is a loving family environment.

An exercise for you is to identify family qualities that you admire. Maybe you admire a family where the spouses work together to take care of the children, or maybe you admire a couple that has great respect and admiration for each other. List those qualities of healthy families and healthy couples and then start to speak and act those qualities into your life.

Here are some qualities of successful couples and families:

1. Common goals and the ability to communicate those goals to one another.

2. Respect: listening to the other non-judgmentally, being emotionally affirming and understanding.

3. Valuing the other person and being able to show that you value him/her.

4. Celebrating birthdays, holidays and developing traditions that make your relationship special.

5. In new relationships, respecting the children and the relationship with the children. Understand that he/she will have his/her children for life. It is a parental relationship, not to be confused with a romantic relationship.

Think of families that you feel are successful and functional, identify those qualities, and start to speak them into your life!

Suicide

> *The dead do not sing praise to the Lord, nor any who go down into silence… But we will bless the Lord from this time forth and forever more…*
>
> Psalm 115:17-18

At age forty-three, I found myself divorced, one daughter living with my ex-husband and one daughter living with me. All I had ever wanted in my life was to have a family that was loving and accepting. I wanted to be part of a family that was fun and a family that was able to celebrate as well as give compassion for sorrow. I wanted a family that respected and loved each other through all difficulties and joys in our lives. That was a desire that I was never to experience, at least at that point in my life. I could not see beyond that point, though. I felt the darkness, the sense of not belonging, of questioning everything that I had ever done, and feeling that I had nothing to give. I was all given out. I gave and gave in my marriage and was met with a brick wall. I fought the greatest battle in my divorce as to not be destroyed and keep some semblance of family for my children. I gave all of that and now at this point in my life, I could not see I had any more to give. Then I sensed something or someone prompting me. It must have been from heaven, I sensed it was telling me, "Chrisanna, choose life, you must choose life, say, 'I choose life!'" So there I went, crying and yelling at the top of my lungs while I drove to work, "I choose life, I choose life, I choose life!"

I have had clients so devastated by their relationship circumstances that they felt the only way out was suicide. Most of my clients talk about feeling that if they just don't wake up in the morning, it would be okay with them. You know Christians do not talk about this; however, suicide is becoming more and more prevalent in our country. I think this is due to losing the support and structure of a functional family system. In not having the support of a strong family, an individual loses his/her sense of reality, becomes overwhelmed and sees no way out of the darkness. I think that suicide as a Christian is actually a soothing thought because when you are so overwhelmed with pain and the darkness is so thick, the thought of being in the arms of Jesus is actually inviting. For some of us, it may be the first set of arms in which we actually find comfort! It is not, however, the path to take. Suicide is actually very selfish. It leaves those who love us devastated. Our pain is relieved, or so we think, and then we leave this legacy of suffering.

There are others who participate in something called "Sub-intentional Suicide;" this is where an individual may neglect his/her health by not taking medications that are needed, participating in risk-taking behaviors, over eating or indulging in alcohol. My prayer for those suffering silently is for them to realize that if someone completes a suicide, then he/she will never have a chance to see how God works out his/her life! They are losing their perspective that this is all just temporary anyway and we have a God who can part the Red Sea (El- Shaddai). In Nathan Stone's book, *Names of God*, he writes, "Elohim is the God who creates nature so that it continues, El-Shaddai is the God who compels nature to do what is contrary to itself." So if He can part the Red Sea for the Israelites, then he can work out any circumstances that fall in our lives! It is assured that Jesus understands our pain as He walked on this earth as a man for thirty-three years and died on the cross for us. As human beings we can feel the pain; learn, grow and become changed by it, or we can allow the pain to consume us! You will find that being thankful for all circumstances and asking God to show you what you need to learn from the circumstance will help to get through the pain. Emotional pain can be as real as physical pain. No, your leg may not be broken; however, your heart is and the pain is very real.

On a very serious note, suicidal ideation, or suicidal thought, starts from one of two treatable diagnoses, and these are either anxiety or depression. Know that anxiety left untreated will turn into depression. It is like the body just cannot take any more stress and it just shuts down. That is when the depression sets in, where you may just not be able to manage your life any longer. Let's look at the symptoms of anxiety and depression as taken from the DSM-IV-TR. This is the manual used to diagnose mental illnesses.

Anxiety

1. Excessive worry and fear that something bad will happen to you or someone close to you. (This should occur for most days for at least six months.)
2. You find it difficult to control the worry.
3. The anxiety or worry are associated with three or more of the following symptoms:

    (a) restlessness or feeling keyed up or on edge

    (b) being easily fatigued

    (c) difficulty concentrating or mind going blank

    (d) irritability

    (e) muscle tension

    (f) sleep disturbance as found in difficulty falling asleep, staying asleep, or in restless, unsatisfying sleep

Depression

1. Showing a depressed mood most of the day, nearly every day, as indicated by either feeling sad, hopeless, empty, or tearful

2. Diminished interest or pleasure in all, or almost all, activities most of the day, nearly every day

3. Significant weight loss or gain

4. Not sleeping or oversleeping

5. Moving either more rapidly or slowly than usual. I ask my clients if they feel like they are moving like a turtle, is it an effort just to get up and get something to drink, shower, put on makeup, etc.

6. Feeling worthless, feeling excessive or inappropriate guilt, nearly every day

7. Diminished ability to think or concentrate, indecisiveness, most days

8. Recurrent thoughts of death, recurrent suicidal ideation without a specific plan, or a suicide attempt or a specific plan for committing suicide

If you recognize these symptoms in yourself, it is time for you to seek treatment. Use this list and highlight your symptoms and then take it to a mental health professional, who will be able to help you.

If you have not treated the underlying anxiety or depression and you are having suicidal thoughts, read the following list.

Mental health tips on suicide:
1. If you are having suicidal feelings or suicidal ideation, without a plan, you need to seek professional help right

away. Remember that depression and anxiety have biological basis in the body, meaning a chemical imbalance. There are multiple medical conditions that can mimic depression. You need to get some medication immediately to help you though the pain. Medication will help you to think better and not be so scattered in your thoughts. Medication is okay; you do not have to be on it for the rest of your life, just to get you through the situation. You would take medication for diabetes or high blood pressure right? Why not for your broken heart.

2. If you are actively suicidal and have a plan to complete the suicide, seek professional help immediately. God's plan is for us to live on this earth, until He calls us home. When we feel like there is no more on this earth for us, that is the time that we need to cling so desperately to our Heavenly Father! He will make the way. He will send those heavenly beings to this earth to hold us when we have no human arms to rest in. Remember as my priest reminds us, "God's gift to you is your life; your gift back to God is what you do with that life."

3. A completed suicide opens the way for your children to also commit suicide. The statistics increase for children to commit suicide if a parent or close relative commits suicide. You see, you are teaching your children that it is okay to check out and that this life is not worth living. Sylvia Plath, author of *The Bell Jar*, committed suicide in 1963. Her son, Nicholas Farrar Hughes committed suicide on March 16, 2009. Do you want to leave that legacy in your family? Many times, understanding that one fact has prevented many people from opting out of life. Your children give you a reason to live.

Healing Past Hurts

> *Fear not, for I am with you; be not dismayed, for I am your God. I will strengthen you, Yes, I will help you, I will uphold you with My righteous right hand.*
>
> ISAIAH 41:10

As a divorced Christian and knowing that I needed a family around me, I had no other choice than to look at my parents. I tried to restore the relationship with my brother; however, it was not meant to be. My sister was long gone and I did not even know where she was. I had my parents. How was I to reconcile all the pain and suffering, not only what I received as a child; but also what I caused to my parents in my marriage? What I did not explain was that my then husband never liked my parents. He told me, and a Christian marriage counselor told me that I needed to not include my parents in my family. "They are destructive, Chrisanna," is what my then husband and the Christian marriage counselor told me; and because of that advice I distanced myself from my parents. What I now know is that isolation is a tactic of abusers. A person who is abusive and controlling will isolate the victim; the abuser will not like the victim to have friends or other family members around. This way the abuser has more control over the victim. As you can see in my case, there was a lot of hurt between my parents and me. It was time for me to enter therapy.

Many people grow up being abused or neglected in their families of origin. These wounds affect functioning as adults, and people find it difficult to maintain or develop meaningful relationships. Facing these hurts is difficult because it can bring back the flood of feelings, making you question your reality. Part of healing is to address the abuse and call it what it is. Do not minimize it! I had a client in her forties that came in feeling devastated after remembering her sexual abuse in her family of origin by her uncle and father. She told me that she really did not think that it was abuse and she should not feel so bad, because she was not burned with cigarettes or beaten senseless. This is an example of minimizing the abuse and when you minimize, it is remembered, but the memory is that it wasn't so bad. If it wasn't so bad, then why is it still affecting you as an adult? Why are you still suffering?

Listed below are some ways that children deal with abuse in their families of origin. These coping mechanisms can stay with you into adulthood.

1. Minimize: looking at the abuse as not significant, many of my clients tell me, "It was really not that bad"

2. Denial: denying that the abuse happened

3. Delusion: believing that something else happened and not believing the factual history

4. Suppression: Consciously forgetting about the abuse; however your subconscious remembers and affects the adult behaviors

5. Dissociation: This is actually a split from reality. It manifests itself as a disconnect from thoughts, memories, feelings or actions. I had one client who found himself in his car and had apparently driven by himself to a place that he did not even know. When he came back to reality he had his cell phone and called his wife and so he was safe. Something triggered him to dissociate. In dissociation there may be physical illnesses such as irritable bowel or migraine headaches.

These coping mechanisms can continue into adulthood setting the Adult Child up for unsuccessful relationships. You may continue to minimize abuse that you receive or give. You may be in denial of the status of your relationship or you may detach and leave your partner feeling lonely and abandoned.

So many of my clients ask me, "How do I get rid of this awful feeling?" When the memories surface the best thing to do is seek professional help. Following are exercises that you can do on your own or with a therapist:

Finding a safe place in your mind:

- In this exercise relax in a comfortable position and close your eyes. Start to focus on your breath and imagine your breath coming in through your navel, filling your lungs and exiting through your mouth. Once you feel relaxed and comfortable, imagine in your mind a place where you feel safe. It can be from any point in your life. Think about the smells, the type of light and think about how you feel. When you find a place where you feel safe and protected, imagine the strength that you are gaining from being in that place and relax. Here you can think about the present and feel in control. Your expressions do not have to be panicked; you can formulate your thoughts and move forward.

Write a letter to your abuser:

- In this exercise you can write a letter to the abuser, take it to your therapist and read the letter to an empty chair imagining that your abuser is sitting in that chair. After you read the letter you can tear it up or discard it anyway you choose. One of my clients put her letter through the shredder.

- You see, I think one of the best ways to feel comfortable with yourself and your life is to look back at those times that haunt you, if they have surfaced, and look at yourself as the innocent child that you were. An example here is that of a person who suffered abuse as a child or teen and carried the "shame" through their life. They may feel "bad" or "unworthy" of experiencing happiness as an adult. The perpetrator may have been a family member, a church leader, a neighbor or another. Writing a letter to your abuser telling him/her what you feel may release some of the burden.

- The abuse may have been physical, sexual or emotional; in any case the abuser did not respect or value you. The abuser tried to tear you down, neglect you or manipulate you. All of the abuse had to do with the adult and not you as a child. Let's look at reframing your incident. Tell me, what child is going to look for sex, to be beaten up, called names or be neglected? God equipped children to be dependent on their parents and other adults. He did not create children to have to fend off adults when threatened. So when you write your letter, look at yourself as an Innocent Child. When you can see yourself as an Innocent Child the memories take on a different aspect than a memory of a "bad" child who grew up to be a "bad" adult. You as the child were a victim; the incident had nothing to do with you! The incident had all to do with the dysfunctional issues that the adult was carrying!

- I have a client who suffered sexual abuse from ages five to thirteen. Her perpetrator was a neighbor. She was sought out from other girls because she was very much on her own at a young age. Her mother worked and her father had left the family. She carried with her for an entire lifetime a sense of being not worthy, less than, and had difficulty with trust and emotional intimacy. Finally in her late fifties she wrote out all her memories of the sexual abuse and formulated a letter to the abuser and figuratively brought him into the sessions. As she read the journal entries, she read as if she was reading a story about someone else. After she finished I asked her what she thought and was feeling? She told me that she now sees herself as the "innocent" and that her motives for going back to the abuser were because he offered her gifts. He also told her that she was his "Sweet Girl" and as a child who had lost her father, she so desperately wanted to be a "Sweet Girl" to someone. She was now able to see she was an innocent victim of a sexual predator. She was just a child. As an adult being able to see herself as an Innocent Child, she felt peace and was able to breathe easier for one of the first times in her life! She is now feeling strong enough to let it go, so she can move on in her life with peace.

Journaling:

+ You can also journal situations from your childhood and then re-evaluate them from an adult standpoint. Learn to give yourself the advice that you would give to a friend or your child. Would you tell your child that he/she was the cause of his/her own abuse? Or would you tell your friend or child that the person who abused them had problems and was a sick person? The abuse had nothing to do with the child; he/she was just the victim.

+ Make sure that you seek help immediately if you are struggling so much that you cannot function, because of depression, anxiety or panic. One thing that I have realized in working with Adult Children is that their ability to trust is broken and they need assurances up front and may be hesitant to seek help from a therapist. If the journaling triggers unresolved emotions and you are alone, these "raw" emotions can spiral into hysteria. That is why seeking help is so important. If you cannot find a therapist, then seek out a solid friend, who will not judge you, until you can find a therapist. Know that these steps are a normal part of who you are as an Adult Child. It is OK; as these emotions and feelings are resolved you will be stronger. Remember, you survived all of the abuse, you made it to this point and you have a tremendous amount of strength in you!

Imagine Yourself as God Sees You:

- This is an exercise that I use with clients, because often times they forget that they were created in the likeness of God. Genesis Chapter One tells us that God created Adam and Eve in His image, both male and female. The logic here is that if you are created in the image of God, then you have to have that Godly character somewhere in you. If you have Godly character, and you focus on that instead of the feelings that you carry from your abuse, you will learn to see yourself as God sees you. You do not have to carry the guilt and pain from your past. Remember, as many psychotherapists teach the more shame you carry from your past means that you are carrying that shame for someone else. It is someone else's dysfunctional behavior that you are internalizing, not your own.

- Now write down three times that you showed Godly character. Did you help a friend who was suffering? Did you rearrange your schedule to be with your child when they needed you? Did you go back to pay for the water on the grocery cart that the cashier missed? How do you show your Godly character? So now write your list and tape it up on your bathroom mirror so you can see it first thing in the morning. Then you will read just how God sees you. He sees you as precious in His sight.

Current Relationships

Train up a child in the way he should go And when he is old he will not depart from it.
                                    PROVERBS 22:6

I learned to be compliant and to get out of the way. I learned that going over to my friend's house was better for me when I was a child. I think my mother also knew that it was better for me; she seemed to have an inexhaustible list of friends that she would send me to for the weekend to get me out of the house. Fleeing became a way for me to escape; it protected me from getting hurt. I tried sticking with it in my marriage because that was a vow in front of God. Only that relationship was abusive. From now on, I would stick to my old coping mechanisms and not allow anyone to get too close. When I felt that I was becoming vulnerable, which is what you need to be in order to have an intimate relationship, the fears of my family of origin and my ex-husband triggered my Inner-Child to feel fear. My fear was that my heart would be crushed yet again. I have walked away from possible relationships many times out of fear of being hurt another time. Not too functional! But this is how I protected myself as a child. When I start to feel vulnerable in a relationship, I have some post-trauma stress and flee! Now I understand myself better and know more how I react, so next time I will be able to talk about my feelings and function as an adult instead of an Adult Child. I also have my heavenly angels and a relationship with my Living God. These are spiritual relationships that keep me going. As I fall asleep at night, alone in my bed, I place the cross of my rosary on my heart. For that moment, the broken heart feels whole. I feel the warmth in my abdomen that only comes from the Holy Spirit; it radiates though my whole body. I find peace; I am not running from this relationship. It is a heavenly relationship that will last for all eternity. I find rest.

To survive in the environment in which you grew up, you developed coping mechanisms. Maybe you have learned that if you lied, it would save you from being hit. Maybe you learned to blame others for your mistakes because it would save you from a punitive punishment. Maybe you learned to run and hide under your bed when your alcoholic father became enraged! When situations trigger these feelings from childhood in our adult life, you may have feelings that transport you right back to the age in which you suffered the abuse. You may find that you react as you did as a child; however, this is preventing you from having intimate successful relationships. You actually are going back to the time of the abuse and reacting as the Wounded Child that you are. As an adult, it is important to realize our coping mechanisms, and then when we feel the overwhelming flood of emotions, learn to look at what a healthy adult would do. In essence, *act* instead of *react*. I thought I was healed from my past hurts, and in preparing to do some more in depth clinical work to learn techniques to work with Adult Children, I found that I had one last layer to heal, and that was the physical abuse that I received from my brother. When I recounted the years of physical and emotional abuse, I became frightened of my new relationship, and I did what I did as a child, and that was "run!" These survival mechanisms served me well as a child to protect me from a devastating environment. These survival mechanisms used in adult relationships can be very difficult for the one who is not an Adult Child. Or, if you are in a relationship with another Adult Child, he/she can be devastated because it will bring back feelings in his/her own history. You just need to know that you cannot control everything and difficult situations happen. You need to make sure that you are okay and taking care of yourself. You also need to know that God is with you and God is in control of all things. Remember He parted the Red Sea, so do you think He can repair relationships or give you new healthy ones?

Types of Childhood Survival Mechanisms	*Effect On Adult Partner*
Fleeing	Abandonment
Detachment	Loneliness
Rage	Alienation
Word Manipulation	Distrust

Adults who continue to hold onto the past have a tendency to project those memories and feelings onto new partners. It will take a very committed partner to be with a person in recovery from Childhood Abuse because the road may be rocky. Some people may not have it in them and may not understand the struggles that you face. If you have a partner that can see the good in you, when you cannot see it in yourself, you are very fortunate. I think that these people heal and move into a functional relationship faster. If you do not have a partner and face changing and moving forward by yourself, know that God can be with you as you make mistakes and gain perspective. It is important not to beat yourself up about mistakes and losses; what is important, is that you learn from them and grow. According to Pia Mellody with The Meadows, "Pain is the feeling that takes you to growth and maturity."

Forgiveness

Then Jesus said, "Father forgive them, for they do not know what they do…"

Luke 23:34

I had realized that things were not good in my family where I grew up. As I listened to stories of how my parents grew up, I decided they did only what they knew to survive. They grew up in The Great Depression and suffered untold horrors. They also tried their best to give us all an education, of which I am very grateful. When you took out the alcohol and stresses from work, I saw my parents aging and becoming probably more their true personalities. You see, my father started his sobriety in 1986, and he changed from a rager to a kind man. I never expected my parents to ask forgiveness from me for being such neglectful parents. I know I am one of the blessed ones to have this type of healing. I can only attribute this to God's hand and the work of His angelic creatures that changed circumstances and opened hearts.

∞

It is normal to make mistakes and ask for forgiveness. I am sure that you have said or done some idiotic things and knew that you needed forgiveness. It is easier for someone to forgive you and you to forgive others if there is an understanding of what you or the other person is struggling with and understand the background. One of the techniques in doing psychotherapy is to draw the family system. This is a technique that was developed by Murray Bowen and is called a Genogram. In tracing the family system, you can easily see the transferring of dysfunctional behaviors from one generation to the next.

In this family system drawn to the right, we can see that the identified patient, Matt, was born in 1953 and was a third-generation alcoholic. His father Karl was a raging alcoholic, and his grandfather Jack was a very violent alcoholic, placing Karl under severe emotional and physical abuse. Karl's mother died when Karl was only three years old, placing him with feelings of abandonment. As an adult Karl married Sue and they had three children: Karen, Matt, and Molly. Karl, becoming alcoholic, continued with the raging he learned from his father, promoting physical and emotional abuse on both Matt and Karen. Matt's sisters also had problems in their own adult lives in that they suffered with addictions.

FAMILY SYSTEM DIAGRAM

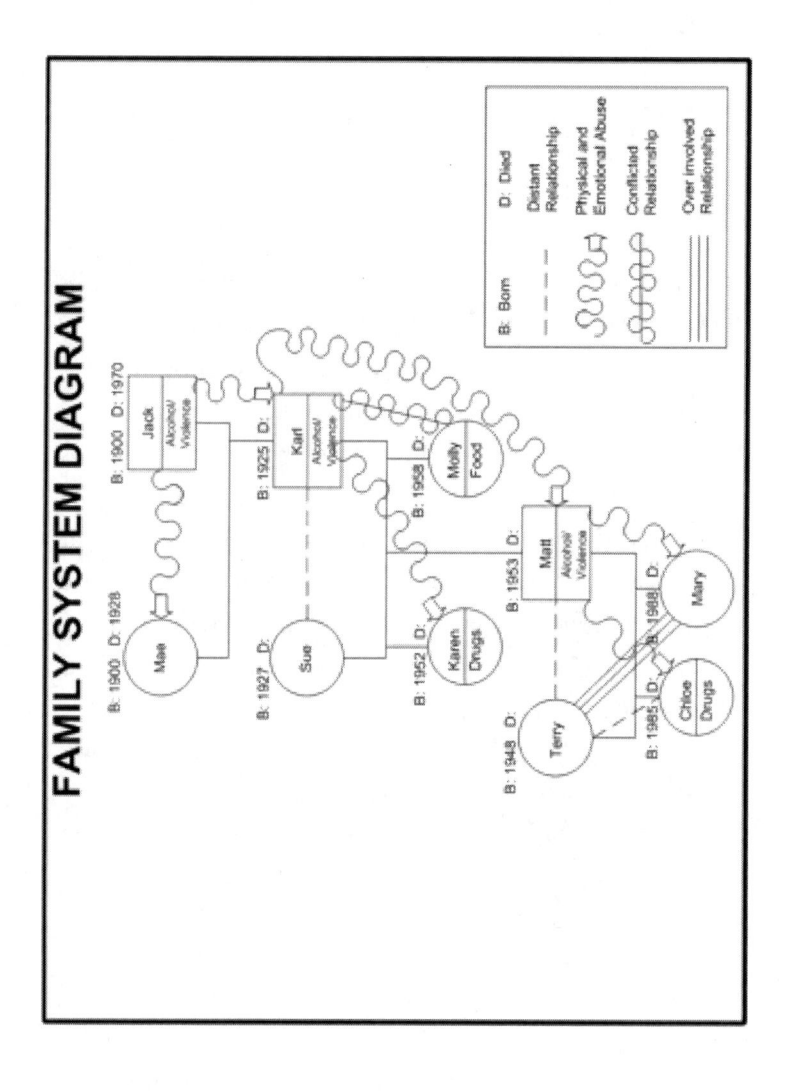

HELD CLOSE BY AN ANGEL

Karen suffered with drugs and Molly with food. Matt's alcoholism prevented him from having a close relationship with his wife, Terry, and he continued the raging with physical and emotional abuse on his daughters Chloe and Mary. Here you can see plain as day the system that Matt grew up in was a sick system, and he continued this sick system in his immediate or nuclear family, placing his daughters and wife at risk for continued dysfunction. You see the person extending the abuse was part of a sick system. If one can never step back and gain a healthy perspective, the sickness goes from generation to generation. The abuse never had anything to do with the child! It was not your responsibility! The abuse was perpetuated when the adult could not take responsibility for his/her actions and was unable to make a change to a more functional way of interacting and relating to his/her family that perpetuated the abuse. And so, we see the same behaviors passed on from one generation to the next. As a functioning adult you must take responsibility for your dysfunction; however, what happened to you as a child never had anything to do with you. Understanding that one concept is freeing and places you to move forward with your life.

You can see in the diagram that with each consecutive generation, the dysfunction gets worse and more severe. The only way to stop the continuation of the abuse is to look at your place in the family history of abuse/dysfunction and start to be functional. Changing behaviors that are a part of you, yet are destructive to you and your relationships takes a lot of work. It is good work to do to move forward and heal.

This is a fictional family; however, it could be any family and many families suffer with generational abuse simply because the sick system becomes what is familiar and the person does not know another way out. There was evil in the system and you, as part of that system, became the victim or the bully as a means to survive. Being able to see the perpetrator as a sick, broken individual releases the power that he/she has over you. He/She was a broken human being who broke your spirit, making you a broken human being. This is where the forgiveness starts, seeing yourself as a victim of a dysfunctional family system. You do not have to continue in that dysfunction, nor continue to be a victim and walk in fear. Identifying the dysfunctional primary relationships from your family of origin and then learning new, healthy ways of relating will bring goodness and growth to you as an individual and to your new relationships. Allow God to touch your heart today, to feel peace.

Attract to Your Level of Individuation

> *Be ye not unequally yoked together with unbelievers for what fellowship hath righteousness with unrighteousness? And what communion hath light with darkness?*
>
> 2 Corinthians 6:14

Twice I attracted men who saw me as an "object." I made their lives more complete, without them having to invest emotionally in my life. I married and then divorced one. Being the "object" was very familiar to me. It was as if my life was not important; after all, I was used to this. My life was a nuisance for my family of origin. As I came to understand relationships through my training, I now know and understand what honoring and loving is all about. Loving takes not only one person investing emotionally; however, it takes both people in the relationship to invest emotionally. As an "object" I could not be loved, because a living human person cannot invest emotionally in an inanimate object. You see, when people love inanimate objects, they lose interest in them. The "object" serves a purpose for a while, and then it is put up on a shelf when it is not needed to serve that purpose, or another "object" takes its place. Because I have developed such a strong loving relationship with Jesus, I now know what it feels like to be loved by Him and now value my life. I know that I am lovable, and that it is functional to be loved and cherished. I feel that I have heavenly beings around me helping me, loving me, because I am a living, breathing creation of my Living God. I now look for a partner that would be comfortable in sharing his life, comfortable in sharing his faith, comfortable in being himself and valuing me, not seeing me as an "object" to take on and off the shelf. What is the shift? I have "individuated," I have matured and grown up. I am no longer functioning as an Adult Child, I have an intimate relationship with Christ, who grounds me and I have a real relationship with the Holy Spirit and then there are those angels, who flutter around me. I do not see them; however, I know they are there.

Who you choose for your mate tells a lot about who you are as a person. Are you choosing a mate out of fear or are you choosing a mate out of wholeness? What does this mean? Individuation means the coming together of different parts to make a whole or complete person. The person can make a healthy separation from the family of origin and no longer have to be defined by that system. This can be a life-long process, especially for Adult Children who struggle with intimacy. Murray Bowen believed individuation started in midlife, and I think that is why I have so many people starting therapy in their forties. Remember, this is a process that continues throughout your life, not an event that happens, and then you are fixed. Individuation comes from realizing the areas in your life that need to be tweaked so you can be more authentic, more intimate in all areas of your personality with another, to include heart, mind, soul, and body. So if you are working just on the surface, you will attract a person who is working just on the surface. If you are making a decision out of fear of being alone or abandoned, then your decisions on your mate are not necessarily the most healthy for you. I tell my clients not to make a decision in their lives based on weakness; always operate from a point of strength. If you are more connected to your heart and feelings and can express these well, you will attract another person that has similar qualities. If you are unsure about what you are feeling, make an appointment with a therapist to discuss your thoughts.

Adult Children can mature every time they experience pain from a situation that triggered a reaction to a buried memory. If you are aware of abnormalities in your behavior, then you can move forward faster. You will be able to identify, connect to the original wound, and address it. This way you will not have to project your negative feelings onto someone else and run the chance of ruining a loving relationship.

Love

We love, because He first loved us...
1 John 4:19

I waited to feel the love he said he professed for me. He told me he loved me, the words. He had the capacity to look into my eyes and say the word love. The cold dark emptiness of his eyes became familiar to me. I thought it was because of his childhood and I could make it better for him. All we needed was to become closer to God as a couple. I continued to have "hope." I prayed for him, getting up at 4:30 in the morning to face east, with my hands raised, crying out to Jehovah–Nissi, the banner of God, who brings victory. I prayed that the scales would fall from my then husband's eyes and he would realize that he had received a gift from God in me and our daughters. I was growing stronger in my faith and understanding what it meant to love, to serve, to be in a family. I realized after my divorce, my ex-husband could not possibly love me or our children. He had not learned how to love himself; he had self-loathing and loathed any person who tried to show him kindness. He did not allow anyone to be close, to share his intimate thoughts. I knew then that for fifteen years I was trying to love a man who could not accept my love, who could not embrace my love. He had no capacity to love. I had never experienced love from a human being. My only example was the one Christ gave to me. That is all I had to go on. The example was that of heavenly beings, the angels, soothing me in the darkness of the night, letting me know that I was loveable. I was loved and cherished by God. What joy! What strength! I could feel the life force that was able to push me forward and touch others whose path crossed mine in this life.

Just what is love? It is such a complicated issue. Healthy love is not controlling or judgmental. It is what changes us to really feel and give freely. Love changes and has different levels of intensity throughout our life. We so desire to be connected to another human being; we are designed that way. Why God made Eve, right? Eve was to be a helpmate to Adam. Understanding the depth and types of love will help you to see love more realistically and also understand that there are different phases of love. Here are some descriptions to help give you a clearer picture. Love is a not a constant; however, it is always moving, progressing, and in healthy relationships getting stronger and more connected.

Paul teaches us about Love in 1 Corinthians chapter 13, telling us about Love in these words:

And if I give all my possessions to feed the poor, and I deliver my body to be burned, but do not have love, it profits me nothing. Love is patient, love is kind, and is not jealous; love does not brag and is not arrogant, does not act unbecomingly; it does not seek its own, it is not provoked, does not take into account a wrong suffered, does not rejoice in unrighteousness, but rejoices with truth; bears all things, believes all things, hopes all things, endures all things. Love never fails… When I was a child, I used to speak as a child, think as a child, reason as a child; when I became a man I did away with childish things. For now we see in a mirror dimly, but then face to face; now I know in part, but then I shall know fully just as I also have been fully known. But now abide faith, hope, love, these three; but the greatest of these is love.

1 Corinthians 13:3-13

The greatest of these is love is very powerful. It is what we are called to do. To love, love our spouses, love our children, and love our neighbors… Love. That is what being a Christian is all about: accepting others, being adult in our relationships. Being able to put yourself in the other's shoes and be able to give to another, and yet if you cannot give, knowing that you can lovingly say that you cannot meet their needs. Trusting that God will bring people into your life in His time to help you develop into the person that He has planned for you to be. Trusting that He made you to be in a relationship and He will not leave you stranded. Trusting that you will be able to walk with another and share a life, loving and honoring in your relationship to feel whole. I imagine that true intimacy comes in being able to accept your partner for every aspect of his/her personality, the good and the ugly. And that he/she will be able to accept all of you as well. Having times in which the relationship is so easy that it is like breathing the same breath. And then there are other times when it is extremely difficult work; however, it is the commitment that takes you to a new level of deeper intimacy to find the same breath again. On a human level we are called to find the intimacy that God so desires with us. St. John Eudes writes:

> He longs to be in you, He wants His breath to be your breath, His heart in your heart, and His soul in your soul.

This to me is true intimacy. Two people who are able to be so connected in honoring each other, in loving each other that they lose sight of themselves at times and see themselves in their Beloved's eyes.

Let these words of C. S. Lewis help you to know what love is all about. As Adult Children we may have never experienced this human love. We are at a loss, we do not know what to do to give love or how to receive love from another. We need a "How to Love for Dummies" book! I love to read, and in reading have learned to incorporate information that I have gathered into my life. I found in reading *The Four Loves*, by C.S. Lewis, descriptions of love that made sense, giving me a sense to define what I was looking for and what was normal or functional. Lewis describes in *The Four Loves* the types of love that make up healthy relationships. We may experience all of these with our mate or we may have other people in our lives to fulfill some of these needs of love.

Affection: …a warm comfortableness, this satisfaction in being together… (C. S. Lewis, *The Four Loves*; pp31-56).

Friendship: sharing in a "collective togetherness," sharing the point of view of "we," "seeing the same truth," "walking side by side." (C. S. Lewis, *The Four Loves*; pp57-90).

Eros: "being in love." Belonging to my *Beloved* and my *Beloved* belonging to me. Of Eros C. S. Lewis writes:

> In the act of love we are not merely ourselves. We are also representatives. It is here no impoverishment but enrichment to be aware that *forces* older and less personal than we work through us. In us all the masculinity and femininity of the world, all that is assailant and responsive, are momentarily focused (C. S. Lewis, *The Four Loves*; pp91-115).

This I see as the work of the Holy Spirit to take a human relationship and make it *holy*. Being face to face, seeing the *other's* soul in his/her eyes and feeling a sense of belonging and safety.

Charity: Describes a love that has *decency* or *common sense*. Charity helps to make the relationship keep the feeling of being *sweet* to honor the other and to be forgiving. (C. S. Lewis, *The Four Loves*; pp116-141).

All four of these types of love exist in this world. Know that if you can exhibit and receive these loves to and from your mate, your beloved, then you will experience a life that will be enriched and authentic. You will be able to have an intimate relationship based on sharing, desire, and belonging. You will put down the childish habits and become a functional adult to share and experience a functional relationship.

The Myth of Eros and Psyche

I love the myth of Eros and Psyche! My friend Stuart said to me, "Is this what you think; love is a myth?" I say to that question, the myth is a love story. It represents the healing power of love and the interaction of angelic forces. I can watch love stories over and over. My favorite is *50 First Dates*, filmed in 2004, with Adam Sandler and Drew Barrymore. I always like when the guy gets the girl and the girl gets the guy as they struggle through their lives. I am a true romantic at heart and so I use this myth, this love story to share with you, to give you hope of finding and attracting the mate that is created for you. Letting you know that even in dire circumstances you can find healing, you can find growth and move to another level of understanding.

Do you remember the story about Eros and Psyche? It is a beautiful love story about chemistry, love, disappointment, separation, appreciation, and finding the "we." Psyche was a beautiful mortal. Eros was the god of love and romance. By means of his arrows, Eros was able to cause anyone he hit to fall in love with the first person seen.

Eros' mother Venus asked Eros to prick Psyche with one of his arrows while Psyche was asleep. Then Venus would place a monster in Eros' place for Psyche to see first and fall in love. Venus was very jealous of Psyche's beauty and did not want her son Eros to fall in love with her and then not be emotionally available for his mother. You see, Venus was displaying highly dysfunctional behavior and mingling her emotions with her son as though she were a jealous lover.

And the story goes, when Eros enters Psyche's room she startles him and looks deeply into his eyes. Eros accidentally pricks himself with one of his arrows and falls deeply in love with Psyche. He goes and tells his mother, and she is enraged. So Venus places a curse on Psyche, which prevents Psyche from having any suitors. Psyche's parents are so concerned that they obtain advice from an oracle, or seer. The oracle tells them that their daughter is too beautiful for a mortal man and her beauty is meant for the gods. Psyche's parents take her up the mountain to leave her to die; however, the West Wind carries Psyche away to a beautiful castle. That night Eros comes in the dark of the night to be with Psyche and they become one, for he desires to be her husband. Eros comes to her every night and demands that she not light a lamp to see who he is until he feels it is appropriate. The West Wind takes Psyche back to visit her sisters and when she tells them the story about her lover, they tell her he is a horrible monster and she must have a lamp and a knife to kill the monster before he kills her. Psyche listens to her sisters (dysfunctional family) and has a knife and lamp ready that night when Eros arrives. Psyche takes the lamp in the middle of the night and looks at Eros, and when she realizes that it is her Beloved Eros, she accidentally pricks herself with one of the arrows and falls deeply in love with him. As she is kissing him, a drop of hot oil from her lamp wakes up Eros and he flies away, leaving broken-hearted Psyche to fall back to earth.

Psyche looks frantically for her Beloved; however, she can find him nowhere. She finally comes to a temple and meets a priest who listens to her story. He tells her that she must go directly and talk with Venus, since Venus started the whole mess. Psyche follows the priest's direction and seeks Venus' help. Venus tells Psyche that she must complete three difficult tasks to earn back her son.

The first is to separate all the grains in a basket before nightfall. Psyche is working frantically and fears she will not finish, when an ant comes with his colony and they easily separate the grains for Psyche. Venus is enraged when she sees that Psyche completed the task.

Venus then tells Psyche that she must collect wool from the golden sheep that graze in a meadow. When Psyche arrives at the meadow a river god tells Psyche that the sheep are ill-natured and will kill her; however, if she waits until the afternoon, she can collect the wool that has pulled off on the bushes. Psyche follows this advice and collects the wool to take to Venus. Again, Venus is enraged at the survival of this mere mortal.

Venus tells Psyche that the stress of caring for her son after Psyche broke his heart has made Venus age. She directs Psyche to go to the Queen of the Underworld and ask Persephone to place some beauty in a box, so that Venus may gain back some of her youthful appearance. Psyche was to bring the box back to Venus. Venus' plan, however, was that Psyche would never return from the Underworld. Psyche decided that the fastest way to the Underworld was to commit suicide and throw herself from a tall tower. To prevent her suicide, the tower speaks to her and tells her the way to the Underworld. The tower then tells Psyche not to eat anything but stale bread or else she would never return to earth. Psyche follows the directions precisely and is successful in bringing the box with beauty back to Venus.

Psyche's interest in the beauty inside the box was getting the better of her and she decided to open it. Instead of beauty she finds that it is an infernal sleep that comes out of the box and overcomes her. Eros, who had forgiven Psyche for her mere humanity, flies to her and revives her with a kiss. She awakes in the arms of Eros and is then taken to Mt. Olympus to become a goddess and marries Eros. There is a beautiful sculpture by Canova that resides in the Louvre in Paris, France. It is named *Psyche Revived by Love's Kiss*. The sculpture by Canova (circa 1787) of this event is pure beauty depicting becoming a "we" through the struggles and misunderstandings of life.

Eros came back and they renewed life in each other. This is a romantic story and it has all the elements of Adult Children who come into a relationship with brokenness from their families of origin. Psyche's parents put her out on a mountaintop and left her to die. (Abandonment) Eros had a mother who was not interested in her son's happiness; however, was concerned with her needs only. Eros listened to his mother even when he was old enough to think for himself. He and his mother had mingled their emotions improperly. This means that the mother did not encourage her son to be himself. She encouraged him to be very dependent on her and she on him for their primary relationship. Psyche was saved by the West Wind, who had mercy on her and sent her to an imaginary castle to protect her. She falls in love with her Beloved, only to listen to the negativity of her sisters that set doubt. She then acted on the fear, costing her the relationship with Eros. After breaking her own heart and the heart of her Beloved, she works very hard to rekindle the relationship. When she thinks she is almost there, she sabotages the relationship again by her curiosity of the beauty that she had in the box. She almost slips away in sleep; however, her Beloved finds her and draws her close even though she has failed him. (He was able to contain her, to see her not only as beautiful but love her for her faults as well as her strengths.) Eros finally had the strength to individuate from his mother and seek his true desires. (He grew up.) His love for her overcame her frailty, her love for him helped him to become a whole person and they breathed life back into each other. They healed each other.

I have a client who experienced this type of love in her life. She was engaged to be married; however, a fear overcame her (stemming from her family of origin), she panicked, breaking off the engagement. Her future husband was a much grounded man and he desired her and saw through the panic, to see the qualities in her that he sought in a wife. He did not let her go, he sought after her, and they now are celebrating thirty-two years of marriage. We talked about how he was able to contain her, to hold her close even though she had flashbacks at times. He provided the safety for her to heal and grow! Remember, a functional family provides safety from the storm for all its members.

Moving forward

> *Then I will make up to you for the years that the swarming locust has eaten...*
>
> JOEL 2:25

I have been single now this year for ten years. My ex-husband left us in 2000. I had a relationship with a man twenty years my senior after my divorce; however, it was not the relationship that was a good fit for me or my daughter. Starting over in midlife is very difficult since you have not only yourself to think about; however, you have your children as well. There have been many times when I thought, well maybe I should just let my heart be hardened and walk in the world. After all, I am already forgiven, so why not just do what our culture tells us is "normal"? Other people do this and they appear happy and can separate out their faith from their behaviors. For me, thank God, I have those heavenly angels who remind me that as a Christian, I am called to walk a different path. My path is lonely on a human level; however it is rich on a spiritual level. I would never trade my relationship with Jesus to have a relationship here on earth that was not heaven-sent. I feel very deeply and experience this life seriously. I have had to find ways to heal without throwing myself immediately into a new relationship. I knew that I wanted to be in a healthier relationship, and so that meant I needed to grow. I needed to understand who I am as a woman of God and what I could bring to a new healthy relationship. Here are ways to help you get over the hurt and pain of your childhood and your past marriage or marriages. Let me help you not to be in pain anymore…

Now that you understand more about yourself and how your life has brought you to this point, you can feel some peace and know you just need more time to develop into the person God planned for you to be. You needed the time to experience the pain and suffering to bring you to a place of self-acceptance and knowing that God *heals the brokenhearted* (Psalm 147:3a). With God on your side, who can lose. Not a one. So let's now look at what it will take for you to move forward. There are seven areas that I will discuss in this chapter, and these are schedule, a support system, proper nutrition, exercise and hobbies, boundaries, and assuring that you take a sexual history prior to starting a new physical relationship leading to marriage.

Schedule:

In starting over, the old schedule has changed. You are moving from doing things with a partner to doing things on your own. A client who just lost his wife of 45 years said to me, "I just don't know what to do. I have always been Faith's husband." There is a time for mourning and a time to move forward; you will know when it is time to move on. Okay, so the first thing is see yourself as an individual, and the healthier you are, the healthier you will attract. So, starting with the basics is important for you to become used to doing things as an individual. Having a daily schedule is very important to keep you moving ahead. A schedule provides a framework for you to have things ready to do when you just cannot think ahead. In any inpatient mental health program, the patients have a schedule. Why do you think this is so? A schedule provides structure, and as human beings, we need it. This structure is especially important when you are going through an adjustment phase from being a couple to being single. If you have a job or career, certainly your work time will take up much of the schedule; however, be sure to plan in some fun things, too. Think of the things that you did as a single person where you felt connected and whole.

One of my clients who was in the Coast Guard started describing his Coast Guard career prior to his marriage. In recounting his experience he felt a sense of joy and acceptance. I noticed that he was smiling when remembering stories. I asked him at the end of the session if there was a voluntary aspect of the Coast Guard that he could join and he said that there was. He knew that the Coast Guard had an Auxiliary. The light bulb went off in his head, I could see it in his eyes, he said, "I can join the Auxiliary!"

It will be painful to start to do things on your own and you will feel that isolating may be easier; however, it is not healthy! Managing any life event is better if you have something to look forward to and knowing what is going to happen next. Planning a schedule around your work, eating proper meals, shopping, cleaning, yard work, hobbies, clubs, church, friends, and family are very important. If there is a show that you want to see, call a friend and ask if he/she wants to go. Identify the times that are most difficult for you. For many single-again people the weekends are the most difficult, as well as holidays. If you are fine with your work schedule from Monday through Friday, then plan activities for the weekend.

One of the most important aspects to your schedule is that you plan time with God. I know you hear this all the time. However, this is your time to connect and receive blessings and grace from your Creator, who desires to be in relationship with you. Do whatever you can do; praying while driving, singing praise songs with your children, listening to Christian radio, or watching a Christian television show. Whatever you can do to connect your life to God the Father, Jesus your Savior, who laid His life down for you, and the Holy Spirit, our Comforter, you must do it. When I take communion in my church I say before I take the Host, "My Lord and My God." I say this because as I take the Host, I know without a doubt I am taking

Christ, my life force. This life force from Christ is one I simply cannot live without.

Positive friends and family:
It is very important to have a support group around you. So many Adult Children find it easier to isolate especially as they age. This is not a healthy behavior since as you isolate, the negative thoughts can ruminate in your mind, bringing you to a clinical level of depression or anxiety. Let's look at family first. If you have repaired the relationships with your family of origin and they are in a healthier state, it is important to keep these relationships. If they are still dysfunctional or actively involved in addiction, then you do not need the negativity around you and it is better to allow God to bring healthy relationships into your life.

In the area of biological family, I know that in instances of incest, estrangement from the family member who perpetrated the abuse is quite normal and healthy. You would not expect a woman or a man who was sexually abused to keep a relationship with the abuser, would you? It is just not normal, the pain is just too much and a constant reminder of the abuse. Estranging or cutting off the relationship with the family member who abused you is okay. It is part of what can be considered positive self-care. Understand you are taking care of yourself so as to not have those negative feelings triggered. If and when you are ready, you can assess if you want to try and repair the relationship. That can be very difficult because the abuser may deny that the abuse happened and you will be back feeling numb because your memory was not affirmed. Take time to get therapy, so you can assess just what are your needs.

This leads us to friends. If you are divorced and the divorce was messy, you may have lost some of the people who you thought were your friends. This is a painful yet common occurrence for people going through divorce. I always say that when you go through a difficult time, your real friends will rise to the surface. So, you may have a handful of friends from your childhood or college days, and renewing those relationships is very important since those people have known you over a long period of time and can be a good support for you. Developing friends at work, through clubs, church, your child's school, or organizations that specialize in single activities are all good places to start to look for new friends. You can also join an Ala-non group if you are not recovering from addictions to develop friendships with people who have struggled with the same issues that you find in yourself. If you are recovering from addictions, it is paramount that you belong to an Alcoholics Anonymous, Narcotics Anonymous, Overeaters Anonymous, Gambling Anonymous, or other recovery group. Finding people whom you have things in common with and can feel a sense of acceptance is very important in your life at this point in time. You want to seek friends who are positive and do not bring you down.

Proper Nutrition
The RD after my name stands for registered dietitian, and I have been practicing for twenty-nine years. So what I tell

you in this section is time tested and true. Proper nutrition is the basis for all human cellular function. You need to eat real food to nourish your body. If you are in your forties or older, you may have noticed that it is more difficult for you to lose weight; this is because as we age, our metabolism slows because we are losing muscle mass.

I teach my clients who want to eat healthily or lose weight to follow a low glycemic nutrition plan. I do not believe in diets, what I teach is a way to eat for the rest of your life. Here is my guidance for proper nutrition and maintaining or losing weight:

1. Avoid processed foods and eat whole foods or foods in their most natural state, no white sugar, white flour, or other processed grains.

2. Non-starchy vegetables are important to eat and have fewer calories; therefore, they are free and you do not have to count them for a serving size.

3. Eat no more than 4 servings of fruit per day. A serving of fruit is one piece of small fresh fruit, ½ of a banana, ½ cup of juice, about 1 ½ cups of fresh berries.

4. Five servings of carbohydrate per day. A serving of carbohydrate counts as a slice of bread, ½ of a bun, ½ of an English Muffin, ½ of a small bagel, ½ cup of potato, pasta, rice or cereal. (Five carbohydrates per day is for weight loss, to maintain your weight allow 6-8 servings of carbohydrate.)

5. Six teaspoons of fats per day, such as olive, canola, safflower oil or butter. For a spread on your toast use real butter (organic if possible due to the hormones and pesticides stored in the animal fat). Do not use low-fat mayonnaise or low fat salad dressing. Your body needs a small amount of fat and when you use the fat free or low fat substitutions, you will not get the fatty acids and your blood sugar level increases leading to extra pounds.

6. Drink 6-8 cups of water per day. Water is important to not only hydrate, it is important to transport your medications and nutrients to the cells. Water also helps to keep your gut functioning better. You can work in your coffee and tea, but make sure you get water in too. If you do not like the taste of plain water, then use some juice that does not contain high fructose corn syrup and put a splash into the water for flavor. Also, diet sodas are not to be consumed if you are not a Diabetic.

7. Do not use artificial sugars if you are not a Diabetic. If your body can tolerate sugar then use 1 teaspoon in your coffee 1-2 times per day. The caloric value of 1 teaspoon of sugar is only 35 calories, so 2 teaspoons per day is not very much in the grand scheme of things.

8. Drink alcohol in moderation. People do not think that liquids have calories. I ask my weight loss clients, "Would you rather drink your calories or eat them?" Most people tell me that they want to chew. So, remember that a four ounce glass of wine has an equivalent

caloric value as one piece of bread. My rule for when you drink wine with a meal is to drink the wine; however, do not eat the bread or any other starch. If you are drinking wine, eat only the protein (meat, fish or poultry) and non-starchy vegetables.

9. Only eat cake or dessert for a birthday, anniversary, or holiday event. Desserts do not need to be a part of your daily food intake. The dessert is only empty calories; it does nothing to nourish your body. Remember, eat to nourish your body; do not eat to nourish your emotions.

10. Start your day with a protein-rich breakfast: eggs, yogurt, cottage cheese, hard cheese, protein drinks, anything that has some protein in it. If you make oatmeal, make it with milk to increase the protein. A bowl of cereal is the worst to eat in the morning, because it is digested so very fast and leaves you hungry. Check yourself midmorning after eating only cereal for breakfast. Are you feeling hungry about midmorning and want to snack on the candy your co-worker has on her desk?

Binge Eating or Binge Drinking:
If you find that you are binge eating or binge drinking alcohol or soft drinks, understand that these behaviors are a way for you to self-medicate, or numb yourself so you do not feel the emotional pain. These types of behaviors do not get you closer to being a whole, functioning adult,

and therefore are counter-productive. The other aspect of binge eating or drinking is that the substance has a tremendous amount of calories, and therefore, you most likely are carrying extra weight. Sugar can be just as addicting as alcohol. Remember, just because you tell yourself that at least you are not drinking; however, you find yourself watching TV with a bag of popcorn, chips, candy, or a pint of ice cream does not make you any less of an addict. Ask yourself these questions and if you respond yes to most of them, I advise you to seek help:

For Food Addiction:

1. Do you spend much of your day thinking about what you will eat next?

2. Do you often eat large amounts of high calorie foods in a short period of time?

3. Do you find yourself sneaking or hiding food?

4. Do you get angry if someone has eaten food that you had planned just for yourself?

5. Do you seek out companions who eat the way you do?

6. Do you find that when you get home you feel like eating anything that is available?

7. Do you find yourself eating out of the container?

8. Has anyone ever told you that you have a problem with food?

9. Do you feel you have a problem with food?

10. Have you tried multiple diets and weight loss products only to lose and put the weight back on again?

There are certainly more characteristics of a food addict; however, if you find you have answered "yes" to half of these questions, you most likely have a food addiction and will need to seek help. Look for counselors in your area who specialize in addictions. You most likely will also want to join an Over Eaters Anonymous group to have some support as you work your recovery. You can also go to my website, www.nutegra.com, to obtain more information on eating disorders and find a link to the USDA Food Guide Pyramid site to obtain a solid meal plan and track your food intake.

For Alcohol Addiction:

These questions are from the CAGE questionnaire, a professional tool used in addressing alcohol use:

- C: Have you ever felt you should *cut* down on your drinking?
- A: Have people *annoyed* you by criticizing your drinking?
- G: Have you ever felt *guilty* about your drinking?
- E: Have you ever had a drink first thing in the morning, *eye opener*, to steady your nerves or get rid of a hangover?

If you answer two or more of these questions with a "yes," then you are probably an alcoholic and need to seek help. If you answered "yes" to one of these questions, then you have a problem and most likely need to seek professional counseling. If you are using or abusing prescription drugs such as Oxycodone, Vicodin, or other prescription painkillers, you can substitute "using" for the word "drinking" in any of the CAGE questions and the same scoring mechanism applies.

Exercise and Hobbies:
Finding the motivation to exercise after the end of a relationship may be very difficult; however, if you do not exercise, you are denying yourself of God-given pain management that is free of charge. You see, as you exercise, your body will release endorphins, which are a natural substance that your body releases to alleviate pain. Endorphins are released after a good work out. Also remember, as we age we will lose our muscle mass. This is a natural occurrence and the only way to assure that you maintain the muscle is to do weight training. Muscle is the part of the body that I call "live tissue" in that is where energy is made or where the calories are burned. Fat does not use energy, fat is stored energy and the only way to reduce fat is to use up more calories than you take in. In order to reduce more calories than you take in there are two components; reducing what you are eating (intake) and then increasing exercising (output). Always check with your doctor before starting an exercise program.

You can use the BMI (Body Mass Index) to tell if you are in shape; however this can be misleading. Let's first look at the BMI. A healthy BMI is anywhere between 18 and 24. A BMI between 25-30 places you in an overweight category. A BMI between 30-35 places you in an Obesity Stage I category. The range of obesity goes up as the BMI increases. Now let's say that the person has large bone structure and large muscle mass. That person may have a higher BMI; however, if the percentage of fat is between 18 and 23 then the person is not overweight or obese. That person is just the way God intended. I use bioelectrical impedance to measure the percentage of body fat, just because I have so many clients that feel so overweight and they become discouraged if they are unable to reach a weight that their doctor is recommending. To illustrate this point I will tell you about a woman who was five eleven and weighed well over 200 pounds. She came to see me for weight loss and she cried telling me about all of the diets that she tried and failed. She told me that her doctor said she needed to weigh 160 pounds and she felt she just could never make it, so she was at her last attempt to lose weight by seeing me. I must tell you this client was not only tall, she was a very large boned woman of Polish and German descent. I did the body composition test and found that her Ideal Body weight was 190 pounds. She told me she thought that she could make that weight and felt such relief. You see, by understanding your body type and composition, you can set realistic goals for yourself. Everyone does not fit into the "box" or the chart on your doctor's wall.

Hobbies are another way to reconnect with yourself. Hobbies are a wonderful way to redirect your painful memories and push you into a positive mindset. Redirecting the pain, anxiety, or depression with a hobby is important to prevent you from going into a downward cycle. Here are just some of the hobbies that my clients have taken up: jewelry-making, stained glass, painting, wood-working, acting, singing, and playing an instrument. Involvements with clubs around your interests are important because they keep you from isolating and keep you around other people. As we age, I have noticed that it is sometimes easier for Adult Children to isolate. This is a very difficult situation, because the sense of hopelessness becomes very strong and prevents you from allowing God to bring about his plan for your life. Remember, God wants to be in relationship with us, and He wants us in relationship with others.

Boundaries:
Boundaries are imaginary lines that we draw on both a physical and emotional level. There are three types of boundaries in families, and these are: rigid, diffuse and flexible. Let's look at these examples:

A rigid boundary is one that does not let anything in or out. The family or individual stays very isolated. Examples of this are families that only socialize with close relatives or limit the interaction with other groups. They do not allow new information to come in or out. An extreme example of a rigid boundary system would be a cult where there are specific rules or specific behaviors that must be followed. Another example is when child abuse is occurring and the family or the member who controls the family, will seek to prevent school officials, police, or medical professionals from getting involved. The exclusion of outsiders allows them to continue the abuse or keep it hidden as a family secret from the outside world. The problem with a rigid boundary is that there is little room for growth, and the members get stifled. They are very suspicious of outside influence and so do not allow information or people to move in and out; therefore, not assessing what is true and not true.

A diffuse family system is one that has few boundaries. This is a family in which everyone knows everyone's business. Relationships are "over-involved." This is where you tell someone something in confidence, and the next thing you know, your brother-in-law finds out about it as well. This is where the single parent allows the children to become best friends and builds his/her life around the children. This is not a healthy system because there are no boundaries, and again, the members of this system cannot grow and develop in a natural process.

A healthy family system boundary is called flexible. A flexible family system will allow people and/or information to come in, process for truth or usefulness, then decide whether to incorporate or discard the new elements. This is a system that allows mistakes, allows information and people to come in and out, and allows for growth in all members of the family. This is a system where adults are adults and children are allowed to be children and do not have to take the place of the missing spouse. This is a family system that is connected and the parents, or caregivers, regulate and guide the family with mutual respect. There is a balance and roles are defined.

We also have boundaries for ourselves. As Adult Children who grew up in one of the first two family systems, rigid or diffuse, we did not learn healthy ways of relating. We grew up forming "walls" to protect our bodies or our hearts, or we grew up "without boundaries" and have experienced abuse and pain of our bodies or our hearts into adulthood. Either way, we find ourselves not feeling good about how we relate to others.

Let's first look at "walls." A person who has a "wall" up physically is someone who does not like to be touched, does not feel comfortable when his/her spouse wants to be intimate, or cannot hug and be spontaneous with his/her children. They may give the child a tap on the back nervously instead of a hug! Many of my clients who are obese have become obese for very specific reasons, and one is so others do not get close to them.

A person can also have an emotional "wall" up. This emotional wall is up to protect them from being hurt emotionally. The problem is that they will never find what it means to be emotionally intimate with a close friend or a mate. This is very sad; they never allow their hearts to be open. Being in a relationship with someone who has a wall up is very difficult because you will never have true intimacy, either physically or emotionally.

C.S. Lewis writes of this state of having a wall around one's heart in *The Four Loves*. The passage follows:

> To love at all is to be vulnerable. Love anything, and your heart will certainly be wrung and possibly broken. If you want to make sure of keeping it intact, you must give your heart to no one, not even to an animal. Wrap it carefully round with hobbies and little luxuries; avoid all entanglements; lock it up safe in the casket or coffin of your selfishness. But in that casket-safe, dark, motionless, airless—it will change. It will not be broken; it will become unbreakable, impenetrable, and irredeemable. The alternative to tragedy, or at least to the risk of tragedy, is damnation. The only place outside of Heaven where you can be perfectly safe from all the dangers and perturbations of love is Hell.
>
> C.S. Lewis, 121

Next is the state of having "no walls" or "no boundaries." This is the person who tells his/her whole life's story the first time that you meet. This is the person who finds him/herself in extramarital affairs because they do not have limits on their behavior. A person can also be without boundaries on an emotional level in that he/she yells and screams and tells you "the truth" as he/she sees it, whether or not it is disrespectful or hurting to the other person. This is the person who cannot say "no" and takes on too much at the risk of neglecting him/herself or his/her family. Having *no boundaries* can look like allowing your children to rule the house. I had one client who gave her son the master bedroom after the divorce and she took another of the bedrooms. This was a family that did not have clear boundaries, and this child was being set up for a false sense of importance. Being "without boundaries" also includes allowing your child of the opposite sex to see you naked on a regular basis or to see you having sex. Not having physical boundaries or emotional boundaries can be very difficult for yourself and your children. It will set up a sense of normalcy for your children that is not normal, and they will continue with the dysfunction in their families. You will be setting your immediate family up for a legacy of disaster.

What are healthy boundaries? Healthy boundaries start with respecting yourself and knowing what are your needs and wants. It starts with defining what type of person you want to be and who you will allow into your world. You may allow some people in and decide it does not feel right and then ask them to leave. It also has to do with being comfortable to express how you feel without yelling, screaming or throwing things. Having healthy boundaries has to do with respecting yourself and others. It is asking yourself, is this person okay to let in, and on what level are they to be included in my life?

To practice talking without blaming someone or yelling at someone, or having *no boundaries*, try using the phrase, "I feel…" when you open the conversation. I feel angry, I feel sad, I feel numb, I feel happy, and I feel disrespected. When you open a conversation with, "I feel" to communicate with other people, you are not attacking them! You are communicating your feelings and this is very empowering. It helps you to feel in control of yourself and safe within a boundary.

Sexual History:
Sexually transmitted diseases are a fact of life in our world today. The increase in infections is staggering and often thought of as just a part of life anymore. This is not what God planned for us and is a result of our fallen world. Many people feel that if they are interested in a person, and the chemistry is right, then sex is a given. The problem is that when you are single again, the new relationship does not have the same innocence as the original marriage. You are therefore exposing yourself to all the people who your intended has been exposed to through his/her previous relationships. To protect yourself and your children, make for sure that you request a sexual history prior to starting a physical relationship. The consequence of not doing this may not be death; however, a long term chronic illness that leads to death, such as HIV-AIDS or Hepatitis C is now considered.

Here are some questions that you can ask your partner or the person whom you desire to be your "beloved." Remember, do not be judgmental of yourself or your prospective mate, since growing up in dysfunctional homes, there may be many unresolved issues around a sexual relationship. These questions can be a way for you to understand your mate on a very intimate level. This information is very personal. Ask these questions at a time when you can be close to each other and have some time to understand and discuss. You can start by stating that you would like to ask some very personal questions because you are attracted to your mate and would like to take the next step toward a solid committed relationship.

1. Are you sexually active?
2. How many partners have you had since your divorce?
3. Were you faithful to your spouse in your marriage?
4. Was your spouse faithful to you?
5. Have you ever contracted a sexually transmitted disease?
6. Have you ever had homosexual sex?
7. Have you ever had unprotected sex outside of your marriage?
8. Are you interested in having children?
9. What type of contraception methods are you interested in using?
10. Have you used intravenous drugs at all in your life?
11. Are you concerned about high risk behaviors? (Unprotected sex, sex with prostitutes, strangers or drug use?)
12. The big question: Are you willing to be tested for HIV, Hepatitis C, and Chlamydia?

After you have the subjective history or the words that your "beloved" is telling you, you must follow it up with blood tests. Have a sexually transmitted disease test to include HIV, Hepatitis C, and Chlamydia. You in turn would need to also provide information so you are transparent as well, by following up with a blood test for your "beloved."

I tell the tragic story about a man who fell in love with a woman after his divorce. He felt that she was the perfect woman for him, funny, attractive and shared his same faith. They married, and about five years into the marriage she started to suffer with symptoms of Hepatitis C. What she did not reveal in the courting aspect of their relationship was that she had worked in the adult entertainment business while she was in college and most likely had been exposed to the Hepatitis C virus at that time of her life. Again, she had been saved by grace; however, we must understand that there are consequences that can last a lifetime and affect others in our family. Tragically, this man also was infected with Hepatitis C and would battle this for the rest of his life. He had children from his first marriage, and so his children would live to see their father have to battle a tragic disease. This was this man and his second wife's "cross to bear" in this world. They would need to do it together, thank God that they both were believers and were able to trust God to work out the rest of their lives. Had they both known their sexual history and had tests prior to marriage or a sexual relationship, this would not have come up as a surprise. Steps could have been taken to protect the spouse without the disease. Someone once said, "Knowledge is powerful."

Remember if the person who you desire to be your "beloved" responds with anger or disgust when you ask the sexual history questions, I would say they do not have your best interest at heart. You will know that they have something to hide and this was not the person God intended for you. If they welcome the opportunity to make you feel comfortable and safe and they expect the same from you, then you have found your partner. A friend of mine once used to describe open communication as "palms up," nothing to hide.

Let's talk about the sexual relationship between you and your beloved. God designed us, both male and female, to be sexual. This is certainly a very private, intimate part of the marriage relationship. If we include God in all areas of our life, then we can see this part of a relationship is also a gift from God. Something I call sacred sexuality. This is really giving your life over to Christ. I truly believe that if you allow God to work in your life, He will bring the perfect person into it. The person He has designed for you on all levels. You certainly must be open for this and be available for God to work in your life. I have seen this in partners where the person found the best one for them to go forward in his/her life. Sacred sexuality happens when your God-given mate will have been praying for you as long as you have been praying for him or her. He/She will know that you are his/her gift from God and you will sense him/her as a gift from God. There will be only going forward. He/She will understand your wounds from your childhood and you will understand his/hers. Both of you will be able to work with each other's wounding and give a sense of safety and peace. You will be each other's Imago, per Harvel Hendricks. A very simplistic way to describe the Imago is a mate that you choose from your subconscious memory of your early caretakers. This relationship is one to help you heal from your childhood wounds, to work out the original wounding, and become a whole person again. Many counselors use myths as a way to illustrate points. In this case, Plato's expression of the Androgen or a being that is whole in their maleness and femaleness is useful. This story can be found in *The Symposium*, written by Plato around 385 BCE. Here is the story:

There were these Beings on earth that were very strong and competent creatures. The little gods like Apollo went to Zeus, up on Mt. Olympus and told Zeus that these beings were going to take over for the gods because they were so powerful. Apollo described these beings as having two heads, four arms, four legs and both male and female parts. They functioned as one and were joined together. They were androgynous beings, two functioning as one, strong and powerful. Apollo was concerned for his place as a god and did not like the perceived competition from these Androgens. Zeus told Apollo, not to worry because in one fell swoop he took his sword and split the Androgen into two. No more competition for the gods. These Androgens were now separated and not as strong. The story goes on to say that we as human beings were those Androgens and we are still now searching frantically for our other half. When we find our androgen, or our other half, we will be whole and healed to our original intention.

Closing

As I look back on my life, I have no other explanation but to thank God that He has always been close to me. I thank God that He loves me and has allowed all the hurt, pain, and abuse in my life to bring me forward to be able to be the person I am today. Had I not experienced what I did in my family of origin, or in my marriage, I would not be able to write this book. I would not be able to relate to my clients as I do. I know that as I narrowly escape an accident as my car stops dead in its tracks, without the usual delay once the brakes are applied, that I have my heavenly angels watching and protecting me. They have been with me from the beginning. We know God is omniscient. He knows past, present, and future. He knew I needed to have angels with me to keep me moving forward. I sense them more now than ever! I know I can never go back in time; I can only go forward now that I understand the past. I know that I have heavenly angelic creatures going forward with me. "Onward," they whisper to me, "Onward; God is not through with you. He has a plan!"

When I tell people that they are "Adult Children," they tell me they have never heard of such a thing. After I read them the list in Chapter Two, they say, "Wow, that's me!" So now you have a sense of yourself and why you "react" they way you do. Being an Adult Child is part of your walk with Christ. It is acknowledging that you are imperfect and in desperate need of a Savior. It is turning every area of your life over to Christ and allowing Him to work things out for you. I always tell my single clients, being lonely in a marriage or a relationship is the worst type of loneliness, because in a marriage we expect to be a couple, we expect to be with our mate. If you are lonely in a marriage, the marriage feels *hopeless*. Being lonely and single is not so bad, because there is always hope that God will bring His choice of a mate into your life so you do not have to settle.

I title this book, *Held Close by an Angel* because as I age, the impact of Christ in my life is very real to me. I have had instances where there was just no other explanation except that it was the work of angels through direction of the Triune God. Like the time we had to leave very quickly because Hurricane Charlie had taken a right turn and was coming right over Punta Gorda. Before we left I prayed that a centurion of angels would protect our home. My daughter placed a can of soda on her window sill before we gathered up our overnight things and our dog, Diana. We left and spent the night in a shelter. Once we returned the next day and my daughter saw the devastation of our little community, she said, "God knows that we need a house to live in Mommy, so I believe that our house will be okay." Don't you know that is exactly what happened? As we drove up to our house, it was wind blown, but intact. We could live in our home as we did the repairs. My daughter's soda can was just where she left it on her windowsill; it had not moved. I thank the centurion of angels that protected our home.

Look for the concrete ways that God is communicating to you. He wants so much to be part of your life. As a single person we need a spouse, we need to be in relationship. Until God brings that human being into your life, allow Him to fill that void.

I see God so much in my life and feel His presence. I think that being a Christian single again makes me depend even more on my God. He tells us that He will care for widows and orphans. Those of us who are divorced have been emotionally widowed, and our children have been emotionally orphaned in many cases. (If you had an amicable divorce, consider yourself very blessed!) He can provide.

People ask me what my marketing plan is for my business. I tell them that I have no big marketing plan; after all, I am a clinician, not a business person. So this is how I market: I stop by my church on the way to my office. Once there, I pray for God's continued favor on my family and my efforts. I then light a candle for my family, my business, my future, and my friends. Placing all things in God's hand takes such a burden off of me! I feel like I am walking with a spring in my step. What was that in the psalm?

"He makes my feet like hinds' feet, and sets me upon my high places" (Psalm 18:33).

Yes, the old cliché is true, "God is good all the time!" He was with you when you were a child, and He is with you now. He cried with you during your childhood, and He is very close to you as an adult. Remember, we are not in Eden anymore and we are not in Heaven yet. Jesus told us …for "the ruler of the world is coming, and he has nothing in Me…" (John 14:30). I take this to mean that Jesus is talking about Satan, who wants to rob us of all joy. There are bad things that happen on this earth. We have a choice to take it personally or see how we can grow from it, and be a better person through it. God wants to take us to a healthier place. He will never leave you or forsake you; He is calling you to heal and be the person He created you to be.

> Do not look forward to the challenges of tomorrow with anxiety, but await them with perfect confidence, so that when they do occur, God, to whom you belong, will deliver you from them. He has kept you up to the present; remain securely in the hand of His providence, and He will help you in all situations. When you cannot walk, He will carry you. Do not think about what will happen tomorrow, for the same Eternal Father who takes care of you today will look out for you tomorrow and always.
> —St. Francis de Sales

Glossary

Adult Child:
An adult who is still operating out of their childhood trauma and unable to have successful adult relationships.

Inner Child:
The abused child that is still traumatized and lives in your heart, mind and soul.

Dysfunctional Family:
A family in which there is not the type of support for all members to develop and grow into functional human beings.

Functional Family:
A family in which all members are supported and loved. There is a flow of communication and all members are respected and their needs are met.

Bibliography

Bishop Verot Catholic High School. Home Page. 14 February 2010 (www.bvhs.org)

Black, Claudia. *It Is Never Too Late to Have a Happy Childhood.*

DeMaria, Rita, Weeks, Gerald and Hof, Larry, *Intergenerational Assessment of Individuals, Couples and Families, Focused Genograms,* Taylor &Francis Group LLC. 1999

Friel, John, Friel, Linda. *An Adult Child's Guide to What's "Normal."* Health Communications, Inc. 1990

Hendrix, Harvel. *Getting the Love You Want a Guide for Couples.* Henry Holt and Company, LLC 1988

Lewis, C. S. *The Four Loves.* New York: Harcourt, Brace, 1960

Lewis, C. S. *The Problem of Pain*. New York, Macmillan, 1962

Mellody, Pia, PIT Training, Phoenix, AZ, October 2009

Wildman, Robert. *The Nutritionist, Food, Nutrition and Optimal Health*. Hayworth Press. 2002